Bethesda

Unit I: Compassion
Student Manual

Created by Jill A. Miller

enter His story

Version 1.0
2014

seeJesus Press

The mission of seeJesus is to help people see and reflect the life, death and resurrection of Jesus through our discipleship resources and training.

seeJesus
P. O. Box 197
Telford, PA 18696
Phone: 215-721-3113
Fax: 215-721-6535

info@seejesus.net
www.seejesus.net

Reminder sheets created by Jill A. Miller
Project Coordinator/Editor: Julie Courtney
Artistic Designer: Seth Guge
Design Coordinator: Liz Voboril
Web Page Designer: Kelly Bergman
Copy Editor: Jane French
Typesetter: Pat Reinheimer

Scripture for
 # Lesson 1

<u>John 13:15</u>

15) I have given you an example to follow. Do as I have done unto you.

Lesson 1 Reminder Sheet

I have given you an example to follow. Do as I have done to you. John 13:15

I can read my Bible.

I can see movies about Jesus.

I can pray.

I love to watch the movie "The Wizard of Oz"! The more I watch it over and over the more I know about Dorothy and that crazy Wizard.

I love Jesus. The more I read the Bible, see movies about Jesus and pray, the more I will know about Jesus and be able to do what he did...I will be able to be like him!

Lesson #1

Scripture for

Lesson 2

Luke 7:11-17

11 Sometime later, Jesus went to a town called Nain. His disciples and a large crowd went along with him.

12 He approached the town gate. Just then, a dead person was being carried out. He was the only son of his mother. She was a widow. A large crowd from the town was with her.

13 When the Lord saw her, he felt sorry for her. So he said, "Don't cry."

14 Then he went up and touched the coffin. Those carrying it stood still. Jesus said, "Young man, I say to you, get up!"

15 The dead man sat up and began to talk. Then Jesus gave him back to his mother.

16 The people were all filled with wonder and praised God. "A great prophet has appeared among us," they said. "God has come to help his people."

17 This news about Jesus spread all through Judea and the whole country.

Lesson 2 Reminder Sheet

Jesus At The Funeral

Jesus looks at the mom...

Jesus shares her sadness...

Jesus wants to make her hurt less.
He wants to comfort her.

Jesus helps her...

Jesus wants me to look at people, comfort them and then help them.

The Picture Communication Symbols ©1981–2013 by DynaVox Mayer-Johnson LLC.
All Rights Reserved Worldwide. Used with permission.

Lesson #2

Scripture for

Lesson 3

Luke 7:11-17

11) Sometime later, Jesus went to a town called Nain. His disciples and a large crowd went along with him.

12) He approached the town gate. Just then, a dead person was being carried out. He was the only son of his mother. She was a widow. A large crowd from the town was with her.

13) When the Lord saw her, he felt sorry for her. So he said, "Don't cry."

14) Then he went up and touched the coffin. Those carrying it stood still. Jesus said, "Young man, I say to you, get up!"

15) The dead man sat up and began to talk. Then Jesus gave him back to his mother.

16) The people were all filled with wonder and praised God. "A great prophet has appeared among us," they said. "God has come to help his people."

17) This news about Jesus spread all through Judea and the whole country.

Lesson 3 Reminder Sheet

The Three Steps of Love

Helping

Sharing peoples' sadness

Looking

The Picture Communication Symbols ©1981–2013 by DynaVox Mayer-Johnson LLC.
All Rights Reserved Worldwide. Used with permission.

Lesson #3

Scripture for

Lesson 4

Luke 10:29-37

29) But the man wanted to make himself look good. So he asked Jesus, "And who is my neighbor?"

30) Jesus replied, "A man was going down from Jerusalem to Jericho. Robbers attacked him. They stripped off his clothes and beat him. Then they went away, leaving him almost dead.

31) A priest happened to be going down that same road. When he saw the man, he passed by on the other side.

32) A Levite also came by. When he saw the man, he passed by on the other side too.

33) But a Samaritan came to the place where the man was. When he saw the man, he felt sorry for him.

34) He went to him, poured olive oil and wine on his wounds and bandaged them. Then he put the man on his own donkey. He took him to an inn and took care of him.

35) The next day he took out two silver coins. He gave them to the owner of the inn. 'Take care of him,' he said. 'When I return, I will pay you back for any extra expense you may have.'

36) "Which of the three do you think was a neighbor to the man who was attacked by robbers?"

37) The authority on the law replied, "The one who felt sorry for him." Jesus told him, "Go and do as he did."

Lesson 4 Reminder Sheet

Slow down

to look and think

about others.

Lesson #4

Scripture for Lesson 5

Luke 10:29-37

29) But the man wanted to make himself look good. So he asked Jesus, "And who is my neighbor?"

30) Jesus replied, "A man was going down from Jerusalem to Jericho. Robbers attacked him. They stripped off his clothes and beat him. Then they went away, leaving him almost dead.

31) A priest happened to be going down that same road. When he saw the man, he passed by on the other side.

32) A Levite also came by. When he saw the man, he passed by on the other side too.

33) But a Samaritan came to the place where the man was. When he saw the man, he felt sorry for him.

34) He went to him, poured olive oil and wine on his wounds and bandaged them. Then he put the man on his own donkey. He took him to an inn and took care of him.

35) The next day he took out two silver coins. He gave them to the owner of the inn. 'Take care of him,' he said. 'When I return, I will pay you back for any extra expense you may have.'

36) "Which of the three do you think was a neighbor to the man who was attacked by robbers?"

37) The authority on the law replied, "The one who felt sorry for him." Jesus told him, "Go and do as he did."

Lesson 5 Reminder Sheet

Jesus treasures me!

I need to treasure others.

The Picture Communication Symbols ©1981–2013 by DynaVox Mayer-Johnson LLC. All Rights Reserved Worldwide. Used with permission.

Lesson #5

Scripture for
 Lesson 6

Luke 15:11-24

11) Jesus continued, "There was a man who had two sons.

12) The younger son spoke to his father. He said, 'Father, give me my share of the family property.' So the father divided his property between his two sons.

13) Not long after that, the younger son packed up all he had. Then he left for a country far away. There he wasted his money on wild living.

14) He spent everything he had. Then the whole country ran low on food. So the son didn't have what he needed.

15) He went to work for someone who lived in that country, who sent him to the fields to feed the pigs.

16) The son wanted to fill his stomach with the food the pigs were eating. But no one gave him anything.

17) Then he began to think clearly again. He said, 'How many of my father's hired workers have more than enough food! But here I am dying from hunger!

18) I will get up and go back to my father. I will say to him, "Father, I have sinned against heaven. And I have sinned against you.

19) I am no longer fit to be called your son. Make me like one of your hired workers.'"

20) So he got up and went to his father. While the son was still a long way off, his father saw him. He was filled with tender love for his son. He ran to him. He threw his arms around him and kissed him.

21) The son said to him, 'Father, I have sinned against heaven and against you. I am no longer fit to be called your son.'

22) But the father said to his servants, 'Quick! Bring the best robe and put it on him. Put a ring on his finger and sandals on his feet.

23) Bring the fattest calf and kill it. Let's have a big dinner and celebrate.

24) This son of mine was dead. And now he is alive again. He was lost. And now he is found.' So they began to celebrate."

In Heaven...

Lesson #6

Jesus will give us new clothes!

Jesus will give us an amazing crown!

We will have an amazing feast!

Scripture for
 Lesson 7

Luke 15:11-24

11) Jesus continued, "There was a man who had two sons.

12) The younger son spoke to his father. He said, 'Father, give me my share of the family property.' So the father divided his property between his two sons.

13) Not long after that, the younger son packed up all he had. Then he left for a country far away. There he wasted his money on wild living.

14) He spent everything he had. Then the whole country ran low on food. So the son didn't have what he needed.

15) He went to work for someone who lived in that country, who sent him to the fields to feed the pigs.

16) The son wanted to fill his stomach with the food the pigs were eating. But no one gave him anything.

17) Then he began to think clearly again. He said, 'How many of my father's hired workers have more than enough food! But here I am dying from hunger!

18) I will get up and go back to my father. I will say to him, "Father, I have sinned against heaven. And I have sinned against you.

19) I am no longer fit to be called your son. Make me like one of your hired workers."'"

---

20) So he got up and went to his father. While the son was still a long way off, his father saw him. He was filled with tender love for his son. He ran to him. He threw his arms around him and kissed him.

21) The son said to him, 'Father, I have sinned against heaven and against you. I am no longer fit to be called your son.'

22) But the father said to his servants, 'Quick! Bring the best robe and put it on him. Put a ring on his finger and sandals on his feet.

23) Bring the fattest calf and kill it. Let's have a big dinner and celebrate.

24) This son of mine was dead. And now he is alive again. He was lost. And now he is found.' So they began to celebrate."

Lesson 7 Reminder Sheet

The Picture Communication Symbols ©1981–2013 by DynaVox Mayer-Johnson LLC.
All Rights Reserved Worldwide. Used with permission.

Lesson #7

Scripture for Lesson 8

John 9:1-7

1) As Jesus went along, he saw a man who was blind. He had been blind since he was born.

2) Jesus' disciples asked him, "Rabbi, who sinned? Was this man born blind because he sinned? Or did his parents sin?"

3) "It isn't because this man sinned," said Jesus. "It isn't because his parents sinned. This happened so that God's work could be shown in his life.

4) While it is still day, we must do the work of the One who sent me. Night is coming. Then no one can work.

5) While I am in the world, I am the light of the world."

6) After he said this, he spit on the ground. He made some mud with the spit. Then he put the mud on the man's eyes.

7) "Go," he told him. "Wash in the Pool of Siloam." Siloam means Sent. So the man went and washed. And he came home able to see.

Lesson 8 Reminder Sheet

Never doubt your value...

All of us must quickly do the jobs God has
assigned us to do. John 9:4

Lesson #8

Scripture for Lesson 9

John 9:8-34

8) His neighbors and those who had earlier seen him begging asked questions. "Isn't this the same man who used to sit and beg?" they asked.

9) Some claimed that he was. Others said, "No. He only looks like him." But the man who had been blind kept saying, "I am the man."

10) "Then how were your eyes opened?" they asked.

11) He replied, "The man they call Jesus made some mud and put it on my eyes. He told me to go to Siloam and wash. So I went and washed. Then I could see."

12) "Where is this man?" they asked him. "I don't know," he said.

13) They brought to the Pharisees the man who had been blind.

14) The day Jesus made the mud and opened the man's eyes was a Sabbath.

15) So the Pharisees also asked him how he was able to see. "He put mud on my eyes," the man replied. "Then I washed. And now I can see."

16) Some of the Pharisees said, "Jesus has not come from God. He does not keep the Sabbath day." But others asked, "How can a sinner do such miraculous signs?" So the Pharisees did not agree with each other.

17) Finally they turned again to the blind man. "What do you have to say about him?" they asked. "It was your eyes he opened." The man replied, "He is a prophet."

18) The Jews still did not believe that the man had been blind and now could see. So they sent for his parents.

19) "Is this your son?" they asked. "Is this the one you say was born blind? How is it that now he can see?"

20) "We know he is our son," the parents answered. "And we know he was born blind.

21) But we don't know how he can now see. And we don't know who opened his eyes. Ask him. He is an adult. He can speak for himself."

22) His parents said this because they were afraid of the Jews. The Jews had already decided that anyone who said Jesus was the Christ would be put out of the synagogue.

23) That was why the man's parents said, "He is an adult. Ask him."

24) Again they called the man who had been blind to come to them. "Give glory to God by telling the truth!" they said. "We know that the man who healed you is a sinner."

25) He replied, "I don't know if he is a sinner or not. I do know one thing. I was blind, but now I can see!"

26) Then they asked him, "What did he do to you? How did he open your eyes?"

27) He answered, "I have already told you. But you didn't listen. Why do you want to hear it again? Do you want to become his disciples too?"

28) Then they began to attack him with their words. "You are this fellow's disciple!" they said. "We are disciples of Moses!

29) We know that God spoke to Moses. But we don't even know where this fellow comes from."

30) The man answered, "That is really surprising! You don't know where he comes from, and yet he opened my eyes.

31) We know that God does not listen to sinners. He listens to godly people who do what he wants them to do.

32) Nobody has ever heard of anyone opening the eyes of a person born blind.

33) If this man had not come from God, he could do nothing."

34) Then the Pharisees replied, "When you were born, you were already deep in sin. How dare you talk like that to us!" And they threw him out of the synagogue.

Lesson 9 Reminder Sheet

Jesus is my friend.

I want to tell my other friends about Him!

Lesson 9

Scripture for
Lesson 10

John 9:8-34

8) *His neighbors and those who had earlier seen him begging asked questions. "Isn't this the same man who used to sit and beg?" they asked.*

9) *Some claimed that he was. Others said, "No. He only looks like him." But the man who had been blind kept saying, "I am the man."*

10) *"Then how were your eyes opened?" they asked.*

11) *He replied, "The man they call Jesus made some mud and put it on my eyes. He told me to go to Siloam and wash. So I went and washed. Then I could see."*

12) *"Where is this man?" they asked him. "I don't know," he said.*

13) *They brought to the Pharisees the man who had been blind.*

14) *The day Jesus made the mud and opened the man's eyes was a Sabbath.*

15) *So the Pharisees also asked him how he was able to see. "He put mud on my eyes," the man replied. "Then I washed. And now I can see."*

16) *Some of the Pharisees said, "Jesus has not come from God. He does not keep the Sabbath day." But others asked, "How can a sinner do such miraculous signs?" So the Pharisees did not agree with each other.*

17) *Finally they turned again to the blind man. "What do you have to say about him?" they asked. "It was your eyes he opened." The man replied, "He is a prophet."*

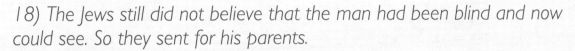

18) The Jews still did not believe that the man had been blind and now could see. So they sent for his parents.

19) "Is this your son?" they asked. "Is this the one you say was born blind? How is it that now he can see?"

20) "We know he is our son," the parents answered. "And we know he was born blind.

21) But we don't know how he can now see. And we don't know who opened his eyes. Ask him. He is an adult. He can speak for himself."

22) His parents said this because they were afraid of the Jews. The Jews had already decided that anyone who said Jesus was the Christ would be put out of the synagogue.

23) That was why the man's parents said, "He is an adult. Ask him."

24) Again they called the man who had been blind to come to them. "Give glory to God by telling the truth!" they said. "We know that the man who healed you is a sinner."

25) He replied, "I don't know if he is a sinner or not. I do know one thing. I was blind, but now I can see!"

26) Then they asked him, "What did he do to you? How did he open your eyes?"

27) He answered, "I have already told you. But you didn't listen. Why do you want to hear it again? Do you want to become his disciples too?"

28) Then they began to attack him with their words. "You are this fellow's disciple!" they said. "We are disciples of Moses!

29) We know that God spoke to Moses. But we don't even know where this fellow comes from."

30) The man answered, "That is really surprising! You don't know where he comes from, and yet he opened my eyes.

31) We know that God does not listen to sinners. He listens to godly people who do what he wants them to do.

32) Nobody has ever heard of anyone opening the eyes of a person born blind.

33) If this man had not come from God, he could do nothing."

34) Then the Pharisees replied, "When you were born, you were already deep in sin. How dare you talk like that to us!" And they threw him out of the synagogue.

I Samuel 16:7

7) But the LORD said to Samuel, "Do not consider how handsome or tall he is. I have not chosen him. I do not look at the things people look at. Man looks at how someone appears on the outside. But I look at what is in the heart."

Lesson 10 Reminder Sheet

The Lord doesn't make decisions the way you do.

People judge others when looking at them.

"Are they pretty, short, wear great clothes?"

But the Lord looks at a person's heart, a person's

thoughts, and what a person really wants to try to do.

I Samuel 16:7

The Picture Communication Symbols ©1981–2013 by DynaVox Mayer-Johnson LLC.
All Rights Reserved Worldwide. Used with permission.

Lesson #10

Unit 1: **Compassion**

Scripture for  Lesson 11

Luke 7: 36-50

36) One of the Pharisees invited Jesus to have dinner with him. So Jesus went to the Pharisee's house. He took a place at the table.

37) There was a woman in that town who had lived a sinful life. She learned that Jesus was eating at the Pharisee's house. So she came with a special sealed jar of perfume.

38) She stood behind Jesus and cried at his feet. She began to wet his feet with her tears. Then she wiped them with her hair. She kissed them and poured perfume on them.

39) The Pharisee who had invited Jesus saw this. He said to himself, "If this man were a prophet, he would know who is touching him. He would know what kind of woman she is. She is a sinner!"

40) Jesus answered him, "Simon, I have something to tell you." Tell me, teacher, " he said.

41) "Two people owed money to a certain lender. One owed him 500 silver coins. The other owed him 50 silver coins.

42) Neither of them had the money to pay him back. So he let them go without paying. Which of them will love him more?"

43) Simon replied, "I suppose the one who owed the most money," "You are right," Jesus said.

44) Then Jesus turned toward the woman. Jesus said to Simon, "Do you see this woman? I came into your house. You did not give me any water to wash my feet. But she wet my feet with her tears and wiped them with her hair.

45) You did not give me a kiss. But this woman has not stopped kissing my feet since I came in.

46) You did not put any olive oil on my head. But she has poured perfume on my feet.

47) So I tell you this. Her many sins have been forgiven. She has loved a lot. But the one who has been forgiven little loves only a little."

48) Then Jesus said to her, "Your sins are forgiven."

49) The other guests began to talk about this among themselves. They said, "Who is this who even forgives sins?"

50) Jesus said to the woman, "Your faith has saved you. Go in peace."

Lesson 11 Reminder Sheet

Jesus is like an xray.

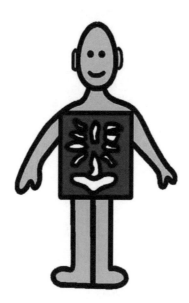

He looks at our insides and fixes us.

Lesson 11

Scripture for Lesson 12

Luke 7:41-48

41) "Two people owed money to a certain lender. One owed him 500 silver coins. The other owed him 50 silver coins.

42) Neither of them had the money to pay him back. So he let them go without paying. Which of them will love him more?"

43) Simon replied, "I suppose the one who owed the most money," "You are right," Jesus said.

44) Then Jesus turned toward the woman. Jesus said to Simon, "Do you see this woman? I came into your house. You did not give me any water to wash my feet. But she wet my feet with her tears and wiped them with her hair.

45) You did not give me a kiss. But this woman has not stopped kissing my feet since I came in.

46) You did not put any olive oil on my head. But she has poured perfume on my feet.

47) So I tell you this. Her many sins have been forgiven. She has loved a lot. But the one who has been forgiven little loves only a little."

48) Then Jesus said to her, "Your sins are forgiven."

Lesson 12 Reminder Sheet

Who does Jesus forgive more?

When I see how much Jesus forgives me, and loves me... I want to love him too, and do what makes him happy.

Lesson #12

Scripture for Lesson 13

Luke 15:28-31

28) "The older brother became angry. He refused to go in. So his father went out and begged him.

29) "But he answered his father, 'Look! All these years I've worked like a slave for you. I have always obeyed your orders. You never gave me even a young goat so I could celebrate with my friends. 30 But this son of yours wasted your money with some prostitutes. Now he comes home. And for him you kill the fattest calf!'

31) "'My son,' the father said, 'you are always with me. Everything I have is yours.

Matthew 6:12-15

12) Forgive us our sins, just as we also have forgiven those who sin against us.

13) Keep us from falling into sin when we are tempted.
Save us from the evil one.'

14) "Forgive people when they sin against you. If you do, your Father who is in heaven will also forgive you. 15 But if you do not forgive people their sins, your Father will not forgive your sins.

Lesson 13 Reminder Sheet

Jesus, please help me forgive others, the way you forgive me.

Forgive us our sins, as we also forgive everyone who sins against us.
Luke 11:4

Lesson #13

Scripture for

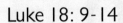 Lesson 14

Luke 18: 9-14

9) *Jesus told a story to some people who were sure they were right with God. They looked down on everybody else.*

10) *He said to them, "Two men went up to the temple to pray. One was a Pharisee. The other was a tax collector.*

11) *"The Pharisee stood up and prayed about himself. 'God, I thank you that I am not like other people,' he said. 'I am not like robbers or those who do other evil things. I am not like those who commit adultery. I am not even like this tax collector.*

12) *I fast twice a week. And I give a tenth of all I get.'*

13) *"But the tax collector stood not very far away. He would not even look up to heaven. He beat his chest and said, 'God, have mercy on me. I am a sinner.'*

14) *"I tell you, the tax collector went home accepted by God. But not the Pharisee. Everyone who lifts himself up will be brought down. And anyone who is brought down will be lifted up."*

The Man God Heard

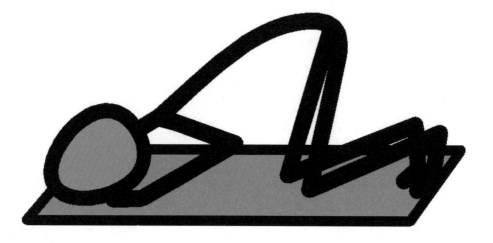

*The Picture Communication Symbols ©1981–2013 by DynaVox Mayer-Johnson LLC.
All Rights Reserved Worldwide. Used with permission.*

Lesson #14

Scripture for

Lesson 15

Luke 18: 9-14

9) *Jesus told a story to some people who were sure they were right with God. They looked down on everybody else.*

10) *He said to them, "Two men went up to the temple to pray. One was a Pharisee. The other was a tax collector.*

11) *"The Pharisee stood up and prayed about himself. 'God, I thank you that I am not like other people,' he said. 'I am not like robbers or those who do other evil things. I am not like those who commit adultery. I am not even like this tax collector.*

12) *I fast twice a week. And I give a tenth of all I get.'*

13) *"But the tax collector stood not very far away. He would not even look up to heaven. He beat his chest and said, 'God, have mercy on me. I am a sinner.'*

14) *"I tell you, the tax collector went home accepted by God. But not the Pharisee. Everyone who lifts himself up will be brought down. And anyone who is brought down will be lifted up."*

Lesson 15 Reminder Sheet

What is inside your cup?

GREED **MEAN**

LOVE **GOODNESS**

JEALOUS **ANGER**

PEACE **PATIENCE**

UNKIND **STEAL**

KINDNESS **JOY**

The picture and communication symbols © 1981-2003 Mayer-Johnson, Inc.
All rights reserved worldwide. Boardmaker ® is a registered trademark.

Lesson 15

Unit I: **Compassion**

Scripture for
Lesson 16

Luke 11:37-43

37) Jesus finished speaking. Then a Pharisee invited him to eat with him. So Jesus went in and took his place at the table.

38) But the Pharisee noticed that Jesus did not wash before the meal. He was surprised.

39) Then the Lord spoke to him. "You Pharisees clean the outside of the cup and dish," he said. "But inside you are full of greed and evil.

40) You foolish people! Didn't the one who made the outside make the inside also?

41) Give to poor people what is inside the dish. Then everything will be clean for you.

42) How terrible it will be for you Pharisees! You give God a tenth of your garden plants, such as mint and rue. But you have forgotten to be fair and to love God. You should have practiced the last things without failing to do the first.

43) How terrible for you Pharisees! You love the most important seats in the synagogues. You love having people greet you in the market places."

Lesson 16 Reminder Sheet

What is the most important thing to me?

schedule

The Picture Communication Symbols ©1981–2013 by DynaVox Mayer-Johnson LLC.
All Rights Reserved Worldwide. Used with permission.

Lesson #16

Scripture for  Lesson 17

Luke 10: 38-42

38) Jesus and his disciples went on their way. Jesus came to a village where a woman named Martha lived. She welcomed him into her home.

39) She had a sister named Mary. Mary sat at the Lord's feet listening to what he said.

40) But Martha was busy with all the things that had to be done. She came to Jesus and said, "Lord, my sister has left me to do the work by myself. Don't you care? Tell her to help me!"

41) "Martha, Martha," the Lord answered. "You are worried and upset about many things.

42) But only one thing is needed. Mary has chosen what is better. And it will not be taken away from her."

Lesson 17 Reminder Sheet

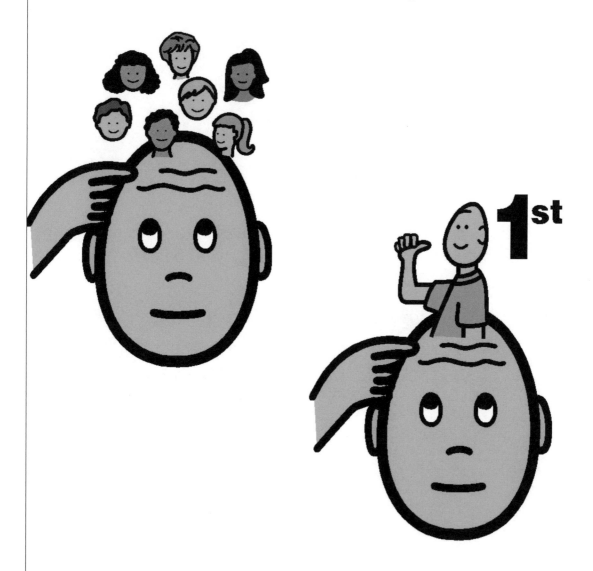

Think about others as much as I think about myself...

The Picture Communication Symbols ©1981–2013 by DynaVox Mayer-Johnson LLC.
All Rights Reserved Worldwide. Used with permission.

Lesson #17

Scripture for

Lesson 18

Mark 8:1-8, Luke 6:31

1) *During those days another large crowd gathered. They had nothing to eat. So Jesus called for his disciples to come to him. He said,*

2) *"I feel deep concern for these people. They have already been with me three days. They don't have anything to eat.*

3) *If I send them away hungry, they will become too weak on their way home. Some of them have come from far away."*

4) *His disciples answered him. "There is nothing here," they said. "Where can anyone get enough bread to feed them?"*

5) *"How many loaves do you have?" Jesus asked. "Seven," they replied.*

6) *He told the crowd to sit down on the ground. He took the seven loaves and gave thanks to God. Then he broke them and gave them to his disciples. They set the loaves down in front of the people.*

7) *The disciples also had a few small fish. Jesus gave thanks for them too. He told the disciples to pass them around.*

8) *The people ate and were satisfied. After that, the disciples picked up seven baskets of leftover pieces.*

Luke 6:31

31) *Do to others as you want them to do to you.*

Lesson 18 Reminder Sheet

I SAY, "Thank you Jesus for dying for me."

I SHOW thank you Jesus by loving others the way you love me.

The Picture Communication Symbols ©1981–2013 by DynaVox Mayer-Johnson LLC.
All Rights Reserved Worldwide. Used with permission.

Lesson 18

Scripture for
Lesson 19

Luke 23:26-49

26) As they led Jesus away, they took hold of Simon. Simon was from Cyrene. He was on his way in from the country. They put a wooden cross on his shoulders. Then they made him carry it behind Jesus.

27) A large number of people followed Jesus. Some were women whose hearts were filled with sorrow. They cried loudly because of him.

28) Jesus turned and said to them, "Daughters of Jerusalem, do not cry for me. Cry for yourselves and for your children.

29) The time will come when you will say, 'Blessed are the women who can't have children! Blessed are those who never gave birth or nursed babies!'

30) It is written, '"The people will say to the mountains, "Fall on us!"   They'll say to the hills, "Cover us!"'"

31) People do these things when trees are green. So what will happen when trees are dry?"

32) Two other men were also led out with Jesus to be killed. Both of them had broken the law.

33) The soldiers brought them to the place called The Skull. There they nailed Jesus to the cross. He hung between the two criminals. One was on his right and one was on his left.

34) Jesus said, "Father, forgive them. They don't know what they are doing." The soldiers divided up his clothes by casting lots.

35) The people stood there watching. The rulers even made fun of Jesus. They said, "He saved others. Let him save himself if he is the Christ of God, the Chosen One."

36) The soldiers also came up and poked fun at him. They offered him wine vinegar.

37) They said, "If you are the king of the Jews, save yourself."

38) A written sign had been placed above him. It read, THIS IS THE KING OF THE JEWS.

39) One of the criminals hanging there made fun of Jesus. He said, "Aren't you the Christ? Save yourself! Save us!"

40) But the other criminal scolded him. "Don't you have any respect for God?" he said. "Remember, you are under the same sentence of death.

41) We are being punished fairly. We are getting just what our actions call for. But this man hasn't done anything wrong."

42) Then he said, "Jesus, remember me when you come into your kingdom."

43) Jesus answered him, "What I'm about to tell you is true. Today you will be with me in paradise."

44) It was now about noon. The whole land was covered with darkness until three o'clock.

45) The sun had stopped shining. The temple curtain was torn in two.

46) Jesus called out in a loud voice, "Father, into your hands I commit my very life." After he said this, he took his last breath.

47) The Roman commander saw what had happened. He praised God and said, "Jesus was surely a man who did what was right."

48) The people had gathered to watch that sight. When they saw what happened, they beat their chests and went away.

49) But all those who knew Jesus stood not very far away, watching those things. They included the women who had followed him from Galilee.

Lesson 19 Reminder Sheet

God, our Father, will give

you another Friend to help you

and to be with you forever.

He lives with you, and he will

be in you. John 14:16,17

Lesson #19

Notes

Notes

Notes

Notes

LOVE WALKED AMONG US

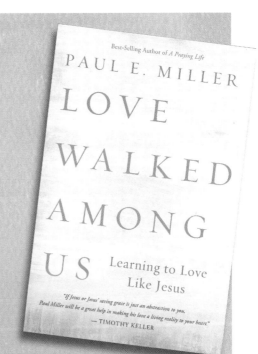

LEARNING TO LOVE LIKE JESUS
BY PAUL MILLER

Paul Miller weaves together stories of his own struggles to love with stories of how Jesus loves. Whether you are a Christian or not yet, your heart will be captured by the wonder of the person of Jesus. This book is based on the corresponding study, *The Person of Jesus*.

Person of Jesus STUDY

How do you love without feeling trapped or used?

How do you balance honesty with compassion?

How do you love when you have problems of your own?

Suitable for discipling or evangelism, *The Person of Jesus* study introduces a Christ so personal, so rich in love that participants are captivated heart-first. Bill, a study leader in Orlando, said, "I've never seen anything like this! I'm enjoying this study as much as a new believer!"

Whether you are looking for a study to invite friends to, or a study for your small groups at church, this is a great tool. Its interactive style engages all participants in a non-threatening way. Designed for first-time through seasoned leaders, this study offers an easy-to-use format, saturated with in-depth content.